Out of the Darkness

The Story of Blacks Moving North, 1890–1940

GREAT JOURNEYS

Out of the Darkness

The Story of Blacks Moving North, 1890–1940

by James Haskins and Kathleen Benson

BENCHMARK BOOKS

MARSHALL CAVENDISH
NEW YORK

To Margaret Emily

With thanks to Michelle Stepto, Yale University, for her careful reading of this manuscript.

Benchmark Books
Marshall Cavendish Corporation
99 White Plains Road
Tarrytown, NY 10591-9001

Cover photograph: *Waiting to move.* Corbis-Bettmann
Photo Research by Candlepants Incorporated
The photographs in this book are used by permission and through the courtesy of;
The Library of Congress: LC-USF34-40828-D, 2-3; LC-USF34-40827-D, 24;
USF33-20598-M1, 26. *Photographs and Prints Division, Schomberg Center for Research in Black Culture, The New York Public Library, Astor, Lenox and Tilden Foundation*: 8 (left), 35 (top & bottom), 37, 47, 51, 54, 60, 67, 96, 104. *The Jones Family*: 8 (right), 73 (top & bottom). *Corbis-Bettmann*: 10, 18, 19, 57, 82, 91, 101, 102. *North Carolina Division of Archives and History*: 12. *South Carolina Library, University of South Carolina, Columbia*: 14. *Mississippi Department of Archives and History*: 17, 21. *UPI/Corbis-Bettmann*: 22, 32 (bottom), 42, 62, 71, 86, 93. *Museum of the City of New York*: 29, 30, 89. *University of Chicago Library, Department of Special Collections*: 32 (top). *Chicago Urban League Records, Special Collections, University Library, University of Illinois at Chicago*: 39. *The National Archives*: neg#86-G-2A-1, 48. *Brown Brothers, Sterling PA*: 66. *Chicago Historical Society/Jun Fujita*: 69. *Frank Driggs/Archive Photos*: 78, 79. *Corbis/Charles Harris; Pittsburgh Courier*: 98. *Celedonia Jones*: 106.

Library of Congress Cataloging-in-Publication Data
Haskins, James, date
Out of the Darkness : the story of Blacks moving North, 1890–1940 / James Haskins and Kathleen Benson
p. cm. — (Great journeys)
Includes bibliographical references and index.
Summary: Uses the experiences of two individuals, Ada "Bricktop" Smith and Joe Jones, to present the story of the Great Migration of Southern Blacks to northern cities from the late 1800s to the years after World War I.
ISBN 0-7614-0970-X
1. Afro-Americans—Migration—History—20th century—Juvenile literature.
2. Afro-Americans—History—1877–1964—Juvenile literature. 3. Afro-Americans—Southern States—History—20th century—Juvenile literature. 4. Rural-urban migration—United States—History—20th century—Juvenile literature. 5. Migration, Internal—United States—History—20th century—Juvenile literature. 6. United States—Race relations—Juvenile literature. 7. Bricktop, 1894— —Juvenile literature. 8. Jones, Joe, 1896–1987—Juvenile literature. [1. Afro-American—Migrations. 2. Afro-Americans—History—1877–1964. 3. Southern States—Race relations. 4. Migration, Internal.] I. Benson, Kathleen. II. Title. III. Series: Great journeys (Benchmark Books (Firm))
E185.6.H34 2000 304.8'089'96073—dc21 99-19882 CIP AC

Printed in the United States of America

1 3 5 6 4 2

Contents

Also by James Haskins

Black, Grey, and Blue: African Americans in the Civil War

The Harlem Renaissance

Get on Board: The Story of the Underground Railroad

One More River to Cross: The Story of Twelve Black Americans

Outward Dreams: Black Inventors and Their Inventions

I Have a Dream: The Life and Words of Martin Luther King, Jr.

Black Dance in America: A History Through Its People

Power to the People: The Rise and Fall of the Black Panther Party

Separate, but Not Equal: The Dream and the Struggle

Also by James Haskins and Kathleen Benson

African Beginnings

Foreword

ADA SMITH WAS BORN IN ALDERSON, WEST VIRGINIA, ON AUGUST 14, 1894. In later years, she was known as Bricktop, and this is the name by which she will be referred to in this book. Bricktop was only four years old when her father, Thomas Smith, died after a series of strokes, leaving his thirty-seven-year-old widow, Hattie Smith, with four children, aged two to fifteen, to support. Hattie Smith did not stay long in Alderson. According to Bricktop, "The town just didn't offer many possibilities for a young widow."

"Chicago was her first and only choice," Bricktop recalled in her autobiography. "Chicago was the home of her Uncle Adam, who was light-complexioned like the rest of her family and who was passing as white. Uncle Adam was a railroad conductor, an unheard-of job for a Negro at that time. Mama made it clear to Uncle Adam that she didn't want to make any trouble. She didn't expect to move in with him. She only wanted to know he was there and that she could count on his help if she needed it. Uncle Adam wrote Mama to come ahead and he'd help her get started."

Joseph William Jones was born in Charleston, South Carolina, on July

*Ada Beatrice Queen Victoria Louise Smith at age
nineteen in Los Angeles. At the time, she had decided
that she needed a more theatrical name, and so she used
Adah when she autographed this picture to her mother.
Her mother wrote back, "Your name is A-D-A."*

*Joseph Jones in 1978. "My father lived to be
ninety," says his son Celedonia, "and he didn't have a
wrinkle on his face or a gray hair on his head."*

10, 1896. Although he was named after his father, he hardly knew him. His mother, Clara Jones, never learned to read and write, and neither did her son, Joe. Although Joe eventually found work in Charleston, like Hattie Smith he also had few choices in the South. After the United States entered World War I in 1917, Joe enlisted in the army and served in France. Discharged when the war was over, Joe returned to Charleston for a time, but soon he moved to New York City to seek greater opportunity.

Bricktop Smith and Joe Jones were only two of thousands of southern African Americans who migrated to the North between the late 1890s and the late 1920s. During that thirty-year period, so many southern blacks moved to the North that the massive relocation came to be called the Great Migration. Although two individuals cannot possibly represent hundreds of thousands of people, through the lens of their unique experiences, the tale of the Great Migration comes to life.

The story of the Great Migration of southern blacks to northern cities from the late 1890s to the post-World War I period is framed here by the experiences of two people: Ada "Bricktop" Smith and Joe Jones.

Ada Smith, who became famous as the international nightclub owner Bricktop, died at the age of eighty-nine in 1984, just months after her autobiography, *Bricktop*, written with Jim Haskins, was published. The material on her life is taken from that book.

Unlike Bricktop, Joe Jones did not become famous. He lived and struggled like most other ordinary African Americans who moved north during the Great Migration. Joe Jones died in 1987. His son Celedonia Jones provided the information on his father for this book—information gleaned not just from memory and family lore but also from research into his family's history.

The authors are grateful both to Ada "Bricktop" Smith and to Celedonia Jones and his family.

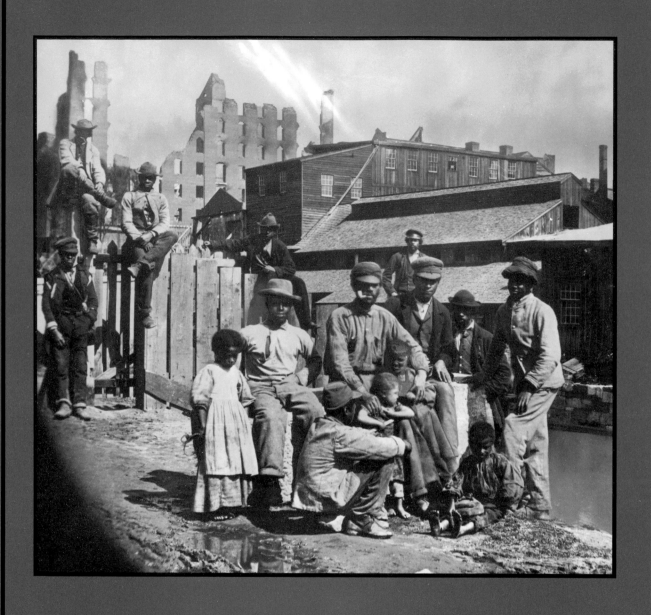

Free, in a late-nineteenth-century southern town.

One

Roots of the Great Migration

ADA "BRICKTOP" SMITH DID NOT KNOW MUCH ABOUT THE ORIGINS OF her father, Thomas Smith, although she believed he was born in slavery. She knew her mother, Hattie Thompson Smith, had been born a slave in 1860 in Virginia. Hattie Thompson Smith's mother was a house slave whose ethnic heritage was mostly Scotch-Irish. According to Bricktop, "her father was probably her mother's master. Whoever my grandfather was, he must have had deep roots in the land, or high social standing. Mama was constantly telling us, 'Don't ever forget you're all FFV [First Families of Virginia] and people expect us to be polite.'" Hattie Thompson was seven-eighths white, with blond hair and gray-blue eyes. According to Bricktop, she could have passed for white if she had wanted to. But she was proud of her heritage and never tried to do so.

Hattie told Bricktop that as a young girl she was sent to Saint Louis to live with her grandmother, who was either white or a light-complected

11

A crew of blacks, supervised by a white man, work on railroad tracks near Spencer, North Carolina, around 1890.

Negro passing for white. The grandmother enrolled Hattie in a Catholic convent school, where she was taught etiquette, manners, and a love of reading—all of which influenced the way she later raised her own children. It is not known what she did after leaving the convent school, but like many other Virginia blacks, after the Civil War she ended up in West Virginia.

West Virginia had been formed during the war. The northwestern counties of Virginia had objected to their state's joining the Confederacy and had chosen instead to remain in the Union. West Virginia was admitted to the Union in 1863, three years after Hattie Thompson was born. After the war, the new state grew quickly. Its railroads and coal mines offered plenty of work, and many blacks migrated there from neighboring states.

Joe Jones hardly knew his father, and it is unlikely that his parents ever married or even lived together. According to federal census records, his mother, Clara Jones, was about twenty-four years old when Joe was born; this places her birth year somewhere around 1875, ten years after the Civil War had ended and slavery had been abolished. But Clara Jones would never know the benefits of real freedom. Dirt poor, she lived in an outbuilding behind someone else's house in the black section of Charleston, South Carolina, and took in laundry to eke out a small living. She never learned to read and write. She was living proof of the broken promises of emancipation.

FOR A GENERATION, there had been hope for southern blacks. After the northern victory in the Civil War, Congress had outlawed slavery and passed a series of constitutional amendments aimed at guaranteeing equal rights for blacks. All three amendments were ratified during Reconstruction, the period of rebuilding in the war-ravaged South. Congress hoped that the former Confederate states would abide by these amendments and treat the newly freed slaves as citizens. But the South

A black section of Charleston, South Carolina, about 1880. Joe Jones's mother lived in a similar alleyway shack.

From Slave to Citizen

THE THIRTEENTH AMENDMENT (1865) outlawed slavery. It stated: "Neither slavery nor involuntary servitude . . . shall exist within the United States, or any place subject to their jurisdiction."

THE FOURTEENTH AMENDMENT (1868) guaranteed citizenship to the former slaves. It defined a citizen of the United States as anyone born or naturalized in the United States and stated: "No State shall make or enforce any law which shall abridge the privileges or immunities of citizens of the United States; nor shall any State deprive any person of life, liberty, or property, without due process of law; nor deny to any person within its jurisdiction the equal protection of the laws."

THE FIFTEENTH AMENDMENT (1870) granted blacks the right to vote: "The right of citizens of the United States to vote shall not be denied or abridged by the United States or by any State on account of race, color, or previous condition of servitude."

had no intention of allowing its freedmen to live free. The southern states tried to get around the Reconstruction Amendments by passing laws called Black Codes. These codes were aimed primarily at stabilizing the workforce—keeping the freedmen on the same land they had cultivated as slaves. But the codes also kept blacks in virtual slavery by denying them the freedom to travel and other basic rights.

In response to this resistance, Congress sent federal troops to occupy the South. They protected the freedmen and established new governments. These governments were unique in several ways, not the least of which was that for the first time African Americans served in them. The governments were also enlightened, in that they attempted to pass legislation that would benefit all, both blacks and whites. Racist caricatures of the time portrayed the Reconstruction legislatures as a bunch of illiterate, corrupt monkeys. Indeed, some members were illiterate, and some were corrupt. But most had a vision of a democratic society in which all could enjoy opportunity. It was these Reconstruction governments that established the first free public education system in the South.

But most white southerners bitterly resented the intrusion of their former northern enemies—not to mention their former slaves—into their affairs. Fights over who would control the governments raged, and the southern economy, which had been devastated by the war, remained in turmoil.

By the early 1870s, many northern whites had grown tired of the continuing unrest in the South and had begun to oppose further federal intervention. The panic of 1873, a severe nationwide depression, helped their cause. More and more, people blamed the country's financial crisis on the political and economic paralysis of the South. The sooner life returns to normal in that part of the country, they said, the better off the entire nation would be. Declare the South "redeemed," they argued. Leave it alone. And if that meant abandoning black southerners to the wrath and resentment of their former owners, so be it.

Though the constitutional amendments passed after the Civil War attempted to guarantee equality for blacks, the South refused to comply. In most areas, libraries were off-limits to blacks, although some cities, such as Greenwood, Mississippi, maintained separate libraries for them. Schools and public transportation were segregated. There were even separate water fountains and rest rooms for blacks.

The South remained in turmoil after the Civil War, as seen in this engraving of a race riot in Charleston, South Carolina, 1866. For a time, the federal government attempted to quell the unrest by sending troops to occupy sections of the former Confederacy. But eventually, northerners abandoned black southerners to the wrath of their former owners.

By April 1877, Republican president Rutherford B. Hayes had pulled out the last remaining federal troops from Louisiana and South Carolina, clearing the way for southern Democrats to regain power and leaving black southerners to fend for themselves. It took some years, but racist southerners eventually dismantled most of the achievements of Reconstruction.

Mississippi was the first state to take the vote from blacks. In 1890, a new state constitution was drawn up. Because the Fifteenth Amendment forbade discrimination on the basis of "race, color, or previous condition of servitude," the framers of the new Mississippi constitution had to find ways to get around it. They instituted a requirement that only those who owned property could vote; a "literacy test," which most blacks could not pass because they had been denied an education; and a poll tax that had to be paid for the right to vote. These requirements effectively disenfranchised the great majority of black voters. When the United States Supreme

The caption for this 1876 engraving reads, "Of course he wants to vote the Democratic ticket!" A so-called democratic reformer says, "You're as free as air, ain't you? Say you are, or I'll blow your black head off!" Through legislation and violence and intimidation, the southern states effectively denied blacks their newly acquired right to vote.

Court upheld what was called the Mississippi Plan, other southern states soon followed suit. By 1910 all had instituted variations of the plan.

But this was not enough for white supremacists in the South. Hand in hand with disenfranchisement came a reinstitution of the Black Codes of the early post–Civil War period. Popularly called Jim Crow laws, they were named after a comic stage character played by a white man in black-face, who based his character on an old black man who did a funny dance. Jim Crow laws introduced segregation into every walk of life. The first of these laws separated blacks and whites on railway cars. The public school systems begun during Reconstruction were cut back or dis-mantled; by the 1880s less than a third of black children received free schooling in the South. Those who did go to school were forced to learn in run-down buildings with few books, from undereducated and under-paid black teachers. Some local laws even went so far as to prevent blacks and whites from playing checkers together in public or looking out the same factory window at the same time.

The denial of voting rights to blacks and the institution of Jim Crow laws were accompanied by a wave of terrible violence against black people in the South. The most horrifying violence was illegal execution by white mobs, or lynching. Between 1890 and 1900, an average of 175 African Americans were lynched every year for the crime of violating the new rules. Usually, the victims were men who overstepped the boundaries imposed upon them by southern society or who had committed some minor transgression. According to Ida B. Wells-Barnett, editor of the Memphis, Tennessee, black newspaper, *Free Speech*, men could be lynched for anything "from violating labor contracts to 'shooting rabbits.'"

Southern blacks protested lynching. They also fought against the creeping segregation that was circumscribing their lives. Beginning in the early 1880s, many challenged the laws in court. The most famous chal-lenge to segregation in the late nineteenth century was brought by Homer Plessy, a light-complected black man who brought suit against

Schools for southern blacks were poorly maintained and staffed and often operated for only a few months a year. During most months, black children were needed to work in the fields.

The most horrifying violence against black people following the Civil War was illegal execution by white mobs, or lynching. Between 1890 and 1910, an average of 175 blacks were lynched every year in the South.

the Lousiana railroad company that forced him to sit in a Jim Crow car. The case of *Plessy* v. *Ferguson* went all the way to the United States Supreme Court, where Plessy's attorneys argued that segregation violated the Thirteenth and Fourteenth Amendments. But on May 18, 1896, a majority of the justices, who were southerners, decided that separate accommodations were constitutional as long as they were "equal." That "separate but equal" decision opened the way for a system of legal segregation in the South that would last for more than sixty years. Bricktop was not yet two years old when that decision was rendered; Joe Jones had just been born.

Hated and constantly violated by southern whites, abandoned by northern whites, the black people of the South were in despair. For many, the only recourse was to leave the land. Like millions of white Americans, they made their way to the growing cities, where jobs were more plentiful and they found some respite in sheer numbers. But the majority of southern black migrants left the South altogether, traveling to northern cities where they might have a chance to live free.

Two distinct routes from the South to the North were born. Blacks from the Mississippi River basin headed to Saint Louis and Chicago, and from there to other inland cities. Blacks from the southern Atlantic coast moved to Philadelphia and New York. People from one town or state tended to gather in those northern cities where their friends and neighbors had already gone. Bricktop's family went to Chicago; Joe Jones went to New York City.

Blacks were not the only Americans to move. The period of industrialization that followed the Civil War led to a nationwide shift from rural to urban life. Before the Civil War, the majority of people in the United States were farmers. They either sharecropped or owned their own land. By the end of the century, the growth of industry had pushed nearly two-thirds of the workforce into nonagricultural occupations. More people were wage earners than were self-employed. People had followed the factories into the country's urban areas, many of which lay in the North. By 1890, one-third of all Americans lived in cities. The modern American city as we know it was born.

In the meantime, an even more massive wave of immigration to the United States was taking place. The largest population movement in human history, it brought ten million foreigners to American shores. Most were from Europe, but they came from Asia and the Caribbean islands as well. Many came because they were forced off the land in their

More than segregation and violence spurred blacks to move to the North. They were part of a nationwide migration from rural to urban areas, as nearly two-thirds of the nation's workforce shifted from farms to factories.

native countries. Millions of Irish Catholics, for example, came as a result of the potato famine of 1845. Others were lured by the promise of opportunity in the United States. The great majority of these immigrants settled in cities. By 1890, eleven American cities had more than a quarter of a million residents. Philadelphia's population was more than one million, and New York's one-and-a-half million.

For American cities straining to accommodate this influx of people, there was no end in sight. And soon, the two waves—southern black migrants and foreign immigrants—would meet, and clash.

Heading north.

Two

The Smiths Go to Chicago

BRICKTOP'S VAGUE MEMORIES OF HER FATHER, THOMAS SMITH, ARE THAT he was a small, dark-skinned man who was slightly hunchbacked and that he operated a barbershop whose clientele was exclusively white. "In those days, you catered either to whites or to blacks. There was no mixing them up," Bricktop explained. She remembered that her father was a deeply religious man, a deacon in a local church, a passionate reader of the Bible, and highly respected by both whites and blacks.

When Bricktop was born on August 14, 1894, her parents, Thomas and Hattie Smith, were living in rooms above a restaurant in Alderson, West Virginia. Bricktop was the youngest of their three girls. Her older sisters were Etta, whose blond hair led to the nickname Blonzetta, and Ethel. Robert was born two years after Bricktop. Bricktop had very pale skin that freckled as she grew older. She also had flaming red hair, which eventually inspired her nickname. At birth, she was named Ada Beatrice

Queen Victoria Louise Virginia Smith. "I don't know who gave me the other names, but Beatrice was to please the pharmacist," Ada later recalled. "Queen Victoria? That was probably Mama's idea. Knowing Mama, she was really thinking big when she put that one in."

After Thomas Smith died, Hattie decided to move the family to Chicago. They went north in two stages. Hattie left first, with Ethel and Robert. Bricktop remained in the care of Blonzetta until Hattie could find a job and set up a new home for the family.

Among the cities of the North, the growth of Chicago had been especially rapid. On the eve of the Civil War, its population had been around 100,000; by 1890, it was more than one million. Nine of every ten inhabitants were either foreign born or second generation (the children of immigrants). By 1900, those foreign immigrants had been joined by a growing number of southern blacks.

It did not take Hattie Smith long to find work. She secured a position with the Applegate family, publishers of the newspaper *Inter-Ocean*. She probably worked as a maid, but she never called herself one. "Whenever she talked about her work," Bricktop remembered, "she referred to herself as 'governess' or 'housekeeper.'"

Hattie Smith had bigger plans than working for someone else. As soon as she had collected her first pay from the Applegates, she looked around for a rooming house to operate. She found one at 171 East Chicago Avenue, over an Italian barbershop. She claimed the large front room and one bedroom for her own family, and soon Blonzetta and Bricktop joined the rest in Chicago.

According to Bricktop, "The East Chicago Avenue place was the first of several that Mama had during the years I was growing up. All were more or less the same. Six or seven rooms. Running water. Inside plumbing in all but one place where we lived. Kerosene lamps. Big iron stove in the kitchen where the water was heated. Mama was a fiend for cleanliness. Seems as if she was always heating water, either for the laun-

Migrant blacks from the South joined immigrants in the burgeoning cities of the North. They lived side by side in neighborhoods where the rents were cheap. Around 1890, the crusading photojournalist Jacob Riis photographed a "Black and Tan" dive on Thompson Street in New York City.

dry or to scrub us in the big wooden tubs in which she washed clothes. . . . Most of my early memories of Chicago begin when we moved to 3237 State Street, way over on the South Side."

Hattie Smith never lacked boarders. In the working-class neighborhoods of Chicago many people rented out rooms in their apartments to the ever-growing number of newcomers. Bricktop described the State Street

In the early years of the black migration, southern blacks and European immigrants mingled, and their children attended school together. This photograph taken by Jacob Riis illustrates the closeness in which the two populations lived.

neighborhood as integrated, with as many Jews, Irish, and Italians as blacks. "The apartment buildings were segregated, but Negro and white buildings stood side by side. When we spilled out into the street each day, we lost sight of color and nationality and behaved like neighbors."

THE MIXED ETHNICITY of the Smiths' neighbors was typical of the time. In 1900, no Chicago neighborhood was more than 10 percent black, and even when the trickle of southern black migrants became a steady flow, blacks were not segregated at first. In fact, according to historian Florette Henri, in 1910, Italian immigrants in Chicago were more segregated than black migrants. The population of Keith School, where Ada enrolled, mirrored the surrounding neighborhood, and the teaching staff was as integrated as the student body.

Like Hattie Smith, many of the women migrants found work in household service or took in laundry. Men were more likely to seek so-called common, or unskilled, labor. Most had been denied an education or the opportunity to learn skills in the South, and they were ill equipped for urban life. But they were beginning to constitute a large enough segment of the city's population to attract people who hoped to harness the political power represented by their sheer numbers.

Ida B. Wells took her antilynching crusade to Chicago. Born in Mississippi in 1862, one year before emancipation, Wells attended a Freedmen's Aid Society school. She moved to Memphis, Tennessee, where she worked as a teacher in a black school. She also began to write for a local black paper, the *Living War*. Eventually, Wells stopped teaching and turned full time to journalism, becoming part owner and editor of the *Free Speech* in the late 1880s. After the lynching in 1892 of three young African-American entrepreneurs by white businessmen who feared their competition, she made the antilynching crusade her own. She editorialized against the lynching and exposed the culprits; this led to the destruction of her printing press by a mob of angry whites.

Ida B. Wells-Barnett made the crusade against lynching her life's work. Beginning her campaign in Memphis, Tennessee, where she was part owner of a newspaper in the late 1880s, she carried her antilynching campaign to New York City and England before moving to Chicago.

A Letter to the President

In 1898, an African-American postmaster was lynched in Lake City, South Carolina. A delegation of Illinois congressmen joined Ida B. Wells-Barnett to write a letter of protest to President William McKinley. That letter read, in part:

Mr. President, The colored citizens of this country in general, and Chicago in particular, desire to respectfully urge that some action be taken by you as chief magistrate of this nation, first for the apprehension and punishment of the lynchers of Postmaster Baker. . . .

For nearly twenty years lynching crimes . . . have been committed and permitted by this Christian nation. Nowhere in the civilized world save the United States of America, do men, possessing all civil and political power, go out in bands of 50 to 5,000 to hunt down, shoot, hang or burn to death a single individual, unarmed and absolutely powerless. Statistics show that nearly 10,000 American citizens have been lynched in the past 20 years. To our appeals for justice the stereotyped reply has been that the government could not interfere in a state matter. Postmaster Baker's case was a federal matter, pure and simple. He died at his post of duty in defense of his country's honor, as truly as did ever a soldier on the field of battle. We refuse to believe this country, so powerful to defend its citizens abroad, is unable to protect its citizens at home.

—from *Who Built America*, Vol. II.,
American Social History Project

The federal government took no action.

Lynching continued for many years in the American South. Like Ida B. Wells-Barnett, these protestors sought federal intervention to stop the illegal executions of southern blacks by white mobs. Washington, D.C., 1922.

Wells was forced to flee Memphis. She carried her crusade to New York, where she wrote for the black newspaper *New York Age* and published a pamphlet entitled *A Red Record*, the first definitive study of lynching in the United States. She traveled to England to raise international support for her campaign, then moved to Chicago, where she organized antilynching clubs for black youth and women. There, she met and married newspaperman Ferdinand Barnett.

In 1905, Robert Abbott founded the *Chicago Defender*, a weekly newspaper that he conceived as a weapon against segregation and discrimination. Born in 1870 in the town of Frederica on Saint Simon Island, off the coast of Georgia, Robert Sengstacke Abbott was the son of former slaves. He attended Hampton Institute in Virginia, where he learned the printing trade. He then moved to Chicago and enrolled in the Kent College of Law. He practiced law for a few years, but he was unable to make a good living at it because whites would not seek the services of a black attorney, and few blacks could afford to pay a lawyer. Eventually, he decided to pursue a career in journalism.

Through the *Defender*, Abbott gave voice to a black point of view at a time when most coverage of blacks by white newspapers was negative. Determined to build the largest circulation of any black newspaper, Abbott crusaded against lynching, the denial of the vote to southern blacks, and many other injustices. The *Defender* was required reading in the homes of literate black Chicagoans. When Abbott began to publish a national edition of the *Defender*, it soon became the newspaper of choice for southern blacks as well. In red ink, the paper screamed out such headlines as 100 NEGROES MURDERED WEEKLY IN UNITED STATES BY WHITE AMERICANS; LYNCHING—A NATIONAL DISGRACE.

Abbott believed that lynching and antiblack rioting were not confined to the American South and that a concerted movement against racism was needed. He was not alone. William E. Burghardt Du Bois, born in Great Barrington, Massachusetts, had earned his Ph.D. from

Robert S. Abbott's weekly newspaper the Chicago Defender *gave voice to a black point of view at a time when most coverage of blacks by white newspapers was negative.*

Abbott was so successful that he soon started publishing a national edition of the Chicago Defender. *He became one of the richest and most influential black men in the nation and a leader in Chicago's black social circles, entertaining frequently at his mansion on South Parkway.*

Harvard University. In 1903, he wrote in *The Souls of Black Folk* that "the problem of the Twentieth Century is the problem of the color line," by which he meant racism in American society. Du Bois was joined by William Monroe Trotter, editor of the *Boston Guardian* (founded in 1901), and others in calling for a meeting in 1905 on the Canadian side of Niagara Falls, a major terminus of the Underground Railroad. The movement that began at that meeting was called the Niagara Movement, after the meeting place. The following year, the group met at Harpers Ferry, West Virginia, the site of the famous raid by the abolitionist John Brown. The Niagara Movement denounced racism and demanded full citizenship rights for blacks. It set forth a militant agenda for change. But it was largely ineffective. It had few dues-paying members. The black press ignored its pronouncements. Whites paid even less attention. Even those whites who were concerned about segregation and racial violence in the South didn't feel the need for a national movement against racism. The problem, they felt, belonged largely to the "backward South."

It took a riot in the summer of 1908 for many whites—and even some northern blacks—to realize that racism plagued the North as well. The riot began after a white woman in Springfield, Illinois, accused a black workman of rape, enraging the local white citizenry, who determined to take the law into their own hands and lynch the accused workman. Springfield authorities spirited the man out of town to protect him from the incensed residents, but this act further infuriated the men of Springfield. A huge white mob went on a rampage, destroying black businesses and homes and killing or injuring black individuals. Two black men were lynched, four whites were killed, and more than seventy people were injured. More than one hundred people were arrested. Five thousand soldiers were required to put down the riot and restore order.

No longer could white reformers dismiss racial violence as belonging uniquely to the South. The Illinois riot had erupted in Springfield, once the home of the Great Emancipator, Abraham Lincoln. Some six

Members of the Niagara Movement pose in front of Niagara Falls in 1905. W. E. B. Du Bois is in the middle row, second from the right, wearing a light-colored hat.

months later, in February 1909, on the one hundredth anniversary of Lincoln's birth, a group of white reformers met in response to the Springfield riot. That same year, the remnants of the Niagara Movement joined forces with this group to form the National Association for the Advancement of Colored People (NAACP). Its agenda included securing the basic citizenship rights guaranteed by the Fourteenth and Fifteenth Amendments, which meant ending segregation laws, ensuring the right to equal education, and guaranteeing the right to vote.

From the beginning, the top echelon of the organization was white; Du Bois was the only African American in the NAACP's inner circle. He founded and served as editor of *The Crisis*, the organization's monthly magazine. But the vast majority of rank-and-file members were black, and by the time the organization was ten years old, many more blacks had moved into leadership positions and local branches had multiplied throughout the North and Midwest.

ALTHOUGH THE SMITH FAMILY read the newspapers, they were personally unaffected by these events. Bricktop was far more interested in show business than in the nation's racial problems. Chicago had a flourishing entertainment industry, and as more and more blacks migrated to the city, an increasing number of theaters and clubs opened for them. Right around the corner from the Smiths was the Pekin Theatre, the first major theater to be devoted to Negro drama. Opened in 1902, it seated about six hundred and soon had its own stock company, the Pekin Players.

Prior to the formation of the Pekin Players in 1906, minstrelsy was the only theatrical form available to blacks. Minstrelsy had its roots in southern plantation slave performances. Every plantation of any size had its talented slave dancers, comedians, and musicians who played the banjo, an instrument brought over from Africa, and the "bones"—animal bones used as clappers. By the early 1800s, some white performers had begun to imitate the blacks. Made up in blackface with burnt cork, they

The influx of southern blacks to Chicago led to the creation of a growing number of businesses to serve them. By the time migration to Chicago peaked in 1923, the city's South Side had become an established black neighborhood.

performed jigs and other dances to popular songs about Negroes. Eventually, these performances evolved into minstrelsy, the first truly American contribution to theater.

By the time blacks were free to form traveling minstrel troupes, the forms of minstrelsy had become so rigidly structured that even they had to perform in blackface. But blacks infused new life into the tired old minstrel formula, adding freshness to the jokes about themselves, introducing new dances, and bringing a new kind of music, based on black folk dancing, that would come to be called ragtime. The seeds of the modern musical comedy were sown when blacks began to enter minstrelsy in large numbers.

The Pekin Players represented a departure from the standard black theatrical fare. They performed what they advertised as "refined white comedies," making up, accordingly, in whiteface.

EVERY CHANCE THEY GOT, the Smith children attended Saturday matinee shows at the Pekin, and by the time she was fourteen, Bricktop wanted to be in show business. She hung around the stage door of the Pekin as often as she could, and from time to time she got work in the chorus. But her mother insisted she stay in school.

When she was sixteen, Bricktop was hired as a member of the chorus to back up the comedy team of Miller and Lyles, who appeared frequently on the Pekin Theatre bill. The duo wanted to take the show on the road, and Bricktop persuaded her mother to let her go with them. For the rest of her life, she would regret not having finished school, but she had been bitten by the show business bug and wanted only to perform on stage.

After a few weeks, the Miller and Lyles show was stranded one hundred miles from Chicago, and Bricktop, who had spent her five-dollar-a-week salary on lodging and food, had to write to her mother to send train fare home. This experience did not dampen her ardor for show business, however, and soon she had joined McCabe's Georgia Troubadours in a tour around Illinois and neighboring states. Subsequently, she joined the Oma Crosby Trio, which performed on the TOBA circuit, the largest Negro traveling entertainment booking agency. The initials stood for Theatre Owners Booking Agency, but black performers joked that they stood for Tough On Black Acts. Eventually, the trio headed east, playing theaters in Pennsylvania before heading to New York City.

In New York, after playing at a series of small houses that catered to blacks, the Oma Crosby Trio secured a booking at Barron's, located in Harlem, on Seventh Avenue and West 134th Street. The club's owner, Barron Wilkins, took to calling Ada "Bricktop" because of her red hair, and the nickname stuck. For the rest of her life, Ada Smith was known as Bricktop.

Bricktop continued working the vaudeville circuits with a series of black acts. She was twenty years old when she returned to Chicago in 1914. World War I had broken out in Europe, but it had not yet begun to affect the average American. Bricktop went to work at the Panama Club on Thirty-fifth and State Street, where she teamed up with two other singers, Cora Green and Florence Mills, to form the Panama Trio. They were a popular act and enjoyed working together at the Panama, but Bricktop soon left the trio and, on her own, went west, first to Saint Paul, Minnesota, and eventually to California. By the time she reached California in 1917, the United States had entered World War I.

Many black migrants found work in northern industries, which were busy producing matériel needed for the United States and its allies during World War I. This photograph shows a riveting crew at the Bethlehem Steel Company shipyard in Sparrow Point, Maryland, 1918.

Three

World War I and the Call to Unite

NINETEEN FIFTEEN WAS A WATERSHED YEAR FOR BLACK MIGRATION. Floods and boll weevil infestations of the cotton crops produced hard times in the South, causing some blacks to leave the land for the cities. But the major spur to migration was World War I. Although the United States stayed out of the war for three years, the nation became a major supplier of war matériel to its allies in Europe—primarily England and France. The booming industries of the North were starved for labor. And just when those industries could have absorbed as many foreign immigrant workers as came, that supply was choked off. In part, this was due to the patriotism of immigrants, who returned to Europe to fight for the countries of their birth. Also, tens of thousands of immigrants either enlisted or were drafted into the United States armed services. But more disastrous for the foreign labor supply were restrictive immigration laws passed by Congress. These new restrictions on immigration included the banning of contract labor, by which American companies imported foreign workers. They also included the imposition of a literacy test for new immigrants and the requirement that new immigrants pay a head tax, or fee, to enter the country.

"Factories, mills and workshops that have been closed to us, through necessity are being opened to us. We are to be given a chance. . . . Prejudice vanishes when the almighty dollar is on the wrong side of the balance sheet," Robert Abbott declared in his newspaper, the *Chicago Defender*. As war production in northern cities increased, Abbott urged southern blacks to move to the North. He published migration poems with titles such as "Land of Hope" and "Bound for the Promised Land." Addressing the deeply held religious beliefs of southern blacks and referring to the biblical precedent of the Jews leaving slavery in Egypt for freedom in Canaan, he called the migration of blacks from the South to the North the flight out of Egypt. He paid black Pullman car porters and dining car waiters to pick up bundles of his newspaper in Chicago and drop them along their routes as their trains traversed the South. Black entertainers were another mobile population whose help he enlisted in spreading his newspaper, and its message.

After a time, a number of southern towns prohibited the sale of the paper and confiscated any copies that were found. Blacks found reading the newspaper were suspected of disloyalty and so-called northern fever. But the *Defender* was a lifeline to the black people of the South, and they passed copies from one to the other until the papers were tattered. Even for those who could not read, being seen with a copy of the *Defender* was a status symbol.

In the meantime, relations between the United States and Germany deteriorated rapidly. The sinking of two ships, the American *Lusitania* in May 1915 and the British *Sussex* in March 1916, began to turn the tide of American public opinion toward war. And after Germany announced a renewal of unrestricted submarine warfare in January 1917, President

Woodrow Wilson broke diplomatic relations with that country. Several more United States vessels were sunk, and on April 2, 1917, Wilson asked Congress to declare war on Germany, stating that "the world must be made safe for democracy." War was officially declared on April 6.

The entry of the United States into World War I was good news for Robert Abbott, who saw it as offering even greater opportunities for blacks. He organized what he called a Great Northern Drive, and even set a date, May 15, 1917, for the black people of the South to leave for the "Promised Land" of the North. Thousands of people were inspired to do so, and the migration fed on itself; the more people went, the more wanted to follow them.

As war production in northern factories went into high gear, desperate industrial employers were prepared to do almost anything to get workers. Many began to hire women for traditionally male positions. The number of female railroad workers tripled, and in many cities women were hired as streetcar conductors. But northern women did not enter the workforce in sufficient numbers to solve the labor shortage. Employers were forced to hire blacks. They enlisted the services of labor agents to travel to the South in search of black workers. Some agents offered prepaid train tickets, which were called justice tickets, as an inducement to migrate. Some railroad and steel companies actually sent special trains to the South to collect interested black workers.

In response, southern states and localities adopted regulations making it difficult for the labor agents to operate and levied high fees for their work. The city council of Macon, Georgia, for example, set the fee for operation at $25,000, and further stipulated that agents must be recommended by ten local ministers, ten manufacturers, and twenty-five businessmen. Southerners also engaged in intimidation of would-be migrants. Police visited the railroad stations and arrested on charges of vagrancy anyone attempting to leave. Informal mobs beat up blacks they suspected of trying to leave the South.

Letters from the "Darkness of the South"

Desperate people wrote to the *Chicago Defender* asking for help in getting to the North. Abbott published many of their letters, such as the three below:

ANNISTON, ALA., APRIL 23, 1917.

Dear Sir: Please gave me some infamation about coming north i can do any kind of work from a truck gardin to farming i would like to leave her and i cant make no money to leave i ust make enough to live one please let me here from you at once i want to get where i can put my children in schol.

MOBILE, ALA., APRIL 25, 1917.

Sir: I am a poor woman and have a husband and five children living and three dead one single and two twin girls six months old today and my husband can hardly make bread for them in Mobile. This is my native home but it is not fit to live in just as the *Chicago Defender* say it says the truth and my husband only get $1.50 a day and pays $7.50 a month for house rent and can hardly feed me and his self and children. . . . I want to get out of this dog hold because I don't know what I am raising them up for in this place and I want to get to Chicago where I know they will be raised and my husband crazy to get there because he can get more to raise his children. . . . He get there a while and then he can send for me. . . . No more at present. hoping to hear from you soon from your needed and worried friend.

BHAM, ALA., MAY 1917.

Sir: i am in the darkness of the south and i am trying my best to get out do you no where about i can get a job in new york. I wood be so glad if cood get a good job . . . o please help me to get out of this low down county i am counted no more thin a dog help me please help me o how glad i wood be if some company wood send me a ticket to come and work for them no joking i mean business i work if i can get a good job.

—from *Journal of Negro History*, July and October 1919

This photograph of a poor woman and her children illustrates the despair expressed by so many of the people who wrote to the Chicago Defender *appealing for help in escaping the South.*

The war provided opportunities for more women in the workplace, as this photograph of a garment factory shows.

In the meantime, the fledgling white labor unions in the North, aware that factory owners were in critical need of workers, pressed for increased wages. In response, some factories began to recruit black workers. While some labor unionists were in favor of organizing black workers, most preferred to keep the unions white. Blacks found themselves competing with whites not only for jobs but also for housing and political power (unlike in the South, blacks in the North could vote).

East Saint Louis, Illinois, across the Mississippi River from Saint Louis, was a cauldron of racial and labor tension. A city of about 75,000 people, its black population practically doubled between 1910 and 1917. The new arrivals from the South were crowded into increasingly segregated neighborhoods that could not hold them, and they began to encroach upon the white immigrant neighborhoods. The immigrants feared that their jobs were also at risk. To be sure, some of the black migrants had been brought in by industrial employers to break union strikes in 1916, but this was not the reason most had come. Still, white labor leaders played upon the fears of white workers. They claimed that blacks threatened their jobs and thus their livelihoods and used these fears to organize a union of white workers. After a strike at an aluminum plant was defeated with the use of black strikebreakers, a local union launched a campaign to drive blacks out of town. A shooting incident touched off a bloody riot in June 1917, which resulted in the deaths of forty blacks and nine whites. In the course of a horrifying two days, white mobs invaded black neighborhoods—shooting, beating, and lynching black residents and burning down their homes.

Blacks across the nation were horrified by the East Saint Louis riots. In New York City, 15,000 blacks staged a silent protest march down Fifth Avenue. Kelly Miller, a teacher and major black spokesman, addressed an open letter appealing for federal legislation against mob law and lynching. "The white people of this country are not good enough to govern the Negro," wrote Miller, "the vainglorious boast of Anglo-Saxon superiority will no longer avail to justify these outrages." Referring to President Woodrow Wilson's promise to "make the world safe for democracy," Miller wrote, "If democracy cannot control lawlessness then democracy must be pronounced a failure." Negroes had always given their blood for their country, Miller reminded the president, adding, "The Negro, Mr. President, in this emergency, will stand by you and the nation. Will you and the nation stand by the Negro?" At least for the duration of the war, Miller pointed out, the president could ask Congress for emergency powers to stop lawlessness and violence against blacks. But Wilson did nothing.

Although the East Saint Louis riots were the worst racial outburst of 1917, such violence also flared in other northern industrial areas where large numbers of southern blacks had moved. There were minor conflicts in 1917 in Pittsburgh, Philadelphia, and Homestead, Pennsylvania, and in Weehawken, New Jersey.

There were also racial incidents in southern areas where military bases were located. The most serious of these occurred in Houston, Texas, in July. After a battalion of black soldiers was stationed there, the local white citizenry worried that they might expect equal treatment, and Houston's all-white police force determined to keep the soldiers "in their place." Two separate confrontations between white police and black soldiers led to an explosion of racial violence in the city, bringing death to two black soldiers and seventeen white men. In a court-martial held early in December, thirteen black soldiers were sentenced to death and hanged a few days later, months before their cases reached the judge advocate general for review. In later trials, other black soldiers were sentenced to death, but on the advice of his secretary of war, who investigated the violence and found that its root was "the enforcement of so-called Jim Crow laws," President Wilson commuted most of those death sentences.

Many southern whites declared that blacks should not be stationed on southern bases. But the U.S. military had determined that blacks as

In what was called at the time the largest murder trial in the United States, sixty-four members of the 24th Infantry were tried for mutiny and murder after a tragic confrontation with white Houston police. Thirteen soldiers were sentenced to death and hanged a few days later, months before their cases reached the judge advocate general for review.

well as whites would be drafted, and Congress had passed the Selective Service Act of May 18, 1917, without reference to the race of those to be drafted into the nation's service. And because the temperate southern climate permitted year-round training of draftees, stationing blacks at southern bases was absolutely necessary.

"This Is Our Country"

In the influential organ of the NAACP, *The Crisis*, W. E. B. Du Bois constantly urged Negro patriotism. Here are excerpts from just two of his many editorials:

CLOSE RANKS

. . . . We of the colored race have no ordinary interest in the outcome [of the war]. That which the German power represents today spells death to the aspirations of Negroes and all darker races for equality, freedom and democracy. Let us not hesitate. Let us, while the war lasts, forget our special grievances and close our ranks shoulder to shoulder with our own white fellow citizens and the allied nations that are fighting for democracy. We make no ordinary sacrifice, but we make it gladly and willingly with our eyes lifted to the hills.

—*The Crisis*, vol. xvi, no. 3, p. 111, July 1918

A PHILOSOPHY IN TIME OF WAR

First, This Is Our Country.

We have worked for it, we have suffered for it, we have fought for it; we have made its music, we have tinged its ideals, its poetry, its religion, its dreams; we have reached in this land our highest modern development and nothing, humanly speaking, can prevent us from eventually reaching here the full stature of our manhood. Our country is at war. The war is critical, dangerous and worldwide. If this is OUR country, then this is OUR war. We must fight it with every ounce of blood and treasure.

—*The Crisis*, vol. xvi, no. 4, pp. 164–165, August 1918

Black Americans had mixed feelings about serving in the U.S. military or otherwise supporting the cause of war. Some purchased Liberty Bonds and War Savings Stamps to show their patriotism. These included Robert Abbott, who bought $12,000 worth of bonds, and W. E. B. Du Bois, who wrote an editorial in *The Crisis* urging blacks to buy bonds, save food, and otherwise "close our ranks shoulder to shoulder with our own white fellow citizens." A few black leaders protested the drafting of blacks on the grounds that they would face further discrimination in the army. But most urged black patriotism, and the majority of ordinary blacks heartily supported the war effort. Over 2,000,000 black men registered with the Selective Service System, and about 370,000 were called into active service. By the time the war ended, blacks had served in every branch of the armed forces—but exclusively in segregated conditions and in noncombat roles, although some saw combat nevertheless.

For many young men, service in the military during World War I offered an entry into a larger world. Home would never be the same.

Four

Joe Jones Joins the Army

JOE JONES WAS TWENTY YEARS OLD WHEN THE UNITED STATES DECLARED war on Germany. He had been born into a world much different from Ada Smith's. Although he knew who his father was, he did not have much contact with him. According to family lore, at some point Joseph Jones Sr. left Charleston to go to New York City, although he got side-tracked for a while before he reached his intended destination. When the train on which he was traveling reached Newark, New Jersey, he thought the conductor announced "New York." He mistakenly got off.

Joe's mother, Clara Jones, was too poor to keep all of her children with her. Federal records from 1900 show Clara Jones living with her mother, Katherine Sanders. That census lists Clara Jones as the mother of one child, but no children in the household. However, Joe had an older brother, Cris, and a sister, Eliza, as well as half siblings. The children never lived together under one roof. The local black community, carrying on a long tradition, took in Clara's children as needed. Joe, his siblings, and his half siblings were raised jointly by family and friends.

Like his mother, Joe Jones never learned to read and write, and it is unlikely that he ever attended school. The city of Charleston had few schools for blacks, and those that did exist were in session only during the winter months, from November to February, when there was little work to do on the area's farms. Tall—he was probably close to six feet in height—and weighing about two hundred pounds, Joe Jones was a hard worker. But he was also illiterate and unskilled, and he faced a bleak future with few possibilities to better his life. Determined to make something of himself, he refused to stay in farmwork. By the time he was in his late teens, he had managed to get a job with a local rubber company, where he learned some mechanical skills.

Within months after the United States entered World War I, Joe Jones joined the army. On his enlistment papers, which were filled out at Fort Moultrie, South Carolina, on October 6, 1917, his occupation is listed as mechanic. He elected to have some of his service pay sent to his mother, Clara.

At the time, the U.S. armed forces were segregated, and blacks were not allowed to serve in combat positions. Instead, black soldiers and sailors did support work—digging ditches, transporting materials, serving in kitchens and mess halls. Private Joe Jones was assigned to Company I of the 301st Stevedore Regiment. Although the army denied him the opportunity to fight in the war, it did give Joe Jones a chance to travel abroad. Just a few weeks after he enlisted, he was assigned to the 334th Company Transportation Corps and sent to France on a troop carrier.

Some 50,000 black soldiers—more than one-third of the American troops—fought in Europe, most of them in support of French troops. White army officials were concerned that the French would make the mistake of treating the African Americans as human beings. So they took steps to alienate the French from the black Americans, warning in a leaflet

A detail of American Negro troops engaged in building a railway line from Brest in western France to the front lines. Racism in the army prevented most black soldiers from serving in combat roles during World War I.

circulated in August 1918 entitled "Secret Information Concerning Black Troops" that the French military command should prevent the rise of intimacy between French officers and black American officers, see that French officers did not commend black American officers too highly, and otherwise avoid "spoiling" them. This effort on the part of American military authorities extended as well to ordinary French people, and sought to influence French public opinion so that Negroes would not be accorded social recognition or be accepted as equals.

The most ridiculous rumor started by the American military in France was that blacks were close descendants of monkeys and in fact had tails, which were hidden by their clothing. Joe Jones told his children that the French women he met were curious to know whether or not he actually had a tail.

In spite of the efforts of U.S. military officials, the French treated the black American soldiers fairly, and while serving in support of French troops, some had the opportunity to see combat. The most famous black soldier in World War I was Private Henry Johnson, who enlisted as a member of the Fifteenth National Guard of New York, which during the war became the 369th Infantry. The 369th was the first unit of black combat troops to arrive in Europe, assigned to support French troops. On the night of May 15, 1918, Johnson and fellow private Needham Roberts were on guard duty at an outpost not far from German lines when they personally prevented an enemy sneak attack. The two were the first U.S. soldiers in the war to receive the croix de guerre, France's highest honor for bravery in action.

As a member of the 334th Company Transportation Corps, Joe Jones moved supplies from one battle to another. One of his main duties was to remove the dead from the field. Another of his jobs was to go out among the dead and retrieve their canteens when troop water supplies ran low. Sometimes he had to perform these tasks under fire in the midst of battle, risking his own life. Thus, although he was not allowed to serve in a combat position, he did see combat.

After Germany surrendered, Joe's company was sent back to the United States, their troop ship arriving in New York City in early June 1919. Joe was honorably discharged from the army at Mitchell Field on Long Island, New York, on June 12, having rendered "honest and faithful" service.

Joe Jones did not reenlist in the army. Although he might have wished to do so, the army had no interest in retaining more than the minimum number of black support personnel necessary in peacetime. Joe's twenty-third birthday was just a month away. His whole life was ahead of him. Yet he had not learned to read and write while in the army, and although he had acquired an awareness of the larger world and a few more mechanical skills, he still had few prospects.

Men like Joe Jones who had served their country in World War I had a hard time adjusting to postwar life. It was difficult for those who had been with the French in Europe and gotten a taste of equal treatment to return to the indignities of life in the United States. The adjustment to life after the war was also difficult for those who had not served in the military but who had enjoyed greater job opportunities on the home front while many white workers were at war. Many lost their jobs to returning white soldiers.

When Joe Jones returned to South Carolina, he got a job in Charleston at the Tuxbury phosphate mill and lodged in the home of some fellow workers. All the adults in the household worked at the Tuxbury phosphate mill, which manufactured fertilizer. Jones had honorably served his country in what was called the war to end all wars, and yet his status as a black man in the South was no different from what it had been before the war. He still had no chance of getting a good job. If he married and had a family, his children, if they attended school at all, would go to a "colored" school that had to depend on cast-off books and other supplies from the white schools. He would have to call whites "Miss" and

Black troops return in triumph from Europe.

"Mister," while they could call him "Boy." In France, he had met ordinary French people who had treated him like a human being. He knew that life in the northern United States was not as good as that in France, but he also knew that in the North he might have a chance. So Joe Jones headed north in the early part of 1920. He rented a room from the Phillips family on West 141st Street, in Harlem.

Girls playing after school in Harlem, 1925.

Five

Joe Jones and Bricktop in New York

By THE TIME JOE JONES ARRIVED IN NEW YORK, THAT CITY HAD BECOME as much of a magnet for southern blacks as Chicago had. And Harlem, in the northern part of Manhattan, was fast becoming a mecca for blacks from all over.

Between 1890 and 1910, the number of black New Yorkers nearly tripled. Although the majority were from the American South, some were from the West Indies and Africa. Like the new immigrants from Europe, they crowded into the scattered sections that contained their "kind"—such as Thirty-seventh and Fifty-eighth Streets, between Eighth and Ninth Avenues.

The majority of southern migrants were uneducated people from rural areas. The conditions under which they had lived in the rural South had not prepared them for northern urban life. The African-American sociologist E. Franklin Frazier wrote in the black newspaper *New York Age* that many Negroes were "ignorant and unsophisticated peasant people without experience [in] urban living . . ." They were not used to modern conveniences or modes of transportation. Not having had access to medical facilities, they did not know they could get their babies vaccinated against infectious diseases. Never having been to a dentist, they didn't realize that regular visits to the dentist were essential for good health. And they were more likely when ill to seek the services of "Indian doctors" and faith healers than professional doctors.

The migrants often transplanted their rural customs to the city, going barefoot in warm weather. Women migrants tended to wear aprons and head rags—scarves that northern black women considered symbols of servitude—in public. W. E. B. Du Bois observed that a migrant man was considered rude if he did not give up his seat on a streetcar to a white woman. He pointed out that black men in the South had learned to avoid interaction with white women altogether. Offering a seat to a white woman implied an insistence on his manhood that could get a black man killed.

The National Urban League was established to address the problems of adjustment that southern migrants encountered. Founded in 1910, just a year or so after the NAACP, the league merged two New York City organizations—the National League for the Protection of Colored Women and the Committee on Urban Conditions of Negroes. As time went on, the Urban League added dozens of branches in cities across the country, offering such services as job and housing registries, advice on how to deal with landlords and city officials, and basic information on the workings of so-called modern conveniences that were completely new to southern blacks just off the farm. According to James R. Grossman in his book *A Chance to Make Good: African Americans, 1900–1929*, the

Urban League in Philadelphia offered instructions to women on "the use of gas, electricity, marketing of foods, how to purchase and prepare cheap cuts of meat."

By the time the Urban League was founded, the black sections of Manhattan had become dangerously overcrowded, and tensions between blacks and whites had escalated. At the same time, a real estate bust in Harlem caused desperate white landlords to start renting to blacks. Black religious and cultural organizations soon followed. In less than a decade, all the major black churches in Manhattan had relocated to Harlem. So had the Negro YMCA, the lodges, the fraternities, the social clubs. By 1914, Harlem had become "A Negro City in New York," according to the title of an article in *The Outlook* magazine.

The black writer and intellectual Alain Locke asserted that the coming together of all these people in Harlem created a new sense of identity among them. He would later coin the term *New Negro* in a book of that title and assert that Harlem was the home of the New Negro:

Here in Manhattan is not merely the largest Negro community in the world, but the first concentration in history of so many diverse elements of Negro life. It has attracted the African, the West Indian, the Negro American; has brought together the Negro of the North and the Negro of the South; the man from the city and the man from the town and village; the peasant, the student, the business man, the professional man, artist, poet, musician, adventurer and worker, preacher and criminal, exploiter and social outcast. Each group has come with its own separate motives and for its own special ends, but their greatest experience has been the finding of one another. Proscription and prejudice have thrown these dissimilar elements into a common area of contact and interaction. Within this area, race sympathy and unity have determined a further fusing of sentiment and experience. So what began in

Harlem residents get together for a block party, about 1915. The sheer number of blacks in Harlem provided opportunities for group expression that were very important for the self-esteem of Harlemites.

terms of segregation becomes more and more, as its elements mix and react, the laboratory of a great race-welding. Hitherto, it must be admitted that American Negroes have been a race more in name than in fact, or to be exact, more in sentiment than in experience. The chief bond between them has been that of a common condition rather than a common consciousness; a problem in common rather than a life in common. In Harlem, Negro life is seizing upon its first chances for group expression and self-determination. It is—or promises at least to be—a race capital.

The group expression and self-determination to which Locke referred took many forms. One was a new sense of black nationalism. Certain segments of Harlem's population welcomed the coming of Marcus Garvey, a West Indian by birth, who arrived in Harlem in 1916 to establish a U.S. branch of his Universal Negro Improvement Association (UNIA). His

Marcus Garvey, a West Indian, became the major voice of black nationalism in Harlem after his arrival in 1916. While most American-born black leaders pushed for integration, Garvey emphasized separatism for blacks.

ideas of black nationalism and his belief that the only way Negroes in the United States could enjoy real freedom was to return to their homeland—his "Back to Africa" program—attracted thousands of converts in Harlem and elsewhere. Garvey established a total of thirty UNIA branches across the United States. In many ways, the UNIA was the polar opposite of the Urban League and the NAACP. The UNIA emphasized separatism for blacks while the others stressed integration.

Racial tensions simmered after the war. Friction between whites and blacks in northern cities was exacerbated by the renewed competition for jobs and by the steady inflow of blacks from the South. Throughout the nation, blacks shared a new sense of power. Blacks were concentrated in cities by 1919. Across the country that year, they gathered to celebrate the tricentennial of the arrival of the first Africans in North America at Jamestown, Virginia. So, it is a sad coincidence that the summer of 1919 would become known as the red summer, after race riots erupted in cities across the nation.

The same factors contributed to these riots as to earlier ones, according to historian Florette Henri:

> The harping of the press on black crime, especially sex crimes; the headlining of violence; the corrupt politicians and police; the mutual fear and suspicion between blacks and whites . . . ; the deliberate creation of labor frictions; and the exacerbation of racial violence, once it was under way, by unequal law enforcement. But one striking common characteristic of the 1919 riots . . . was the counterattack of beleaguered black people.

More than twenty riots occurred during the last six months of 1919 in such cities as Boston, Massachusetts; Omaha, Nebraska; Tulsa, Oklahoma; and Washington, D.C. The worst incident took place in Chicago, where during five days of active rioting thirty-eight people died, over five

A mob chasing a black man, who was later stoned to death during antiblack riots in Chicago, 1919.

hundred were injured, some one thousand were left homeless, and approximately $250,000 worth of property was destroyed.

JOE JONES MAY HAVE HEARD of the explosions in northern cities, but they did not deter him from going north. Nor is it likely that he knew much about Marcus Garvey. After moving to New York City, he did not become a Garveyite. According to Joe's daughter Betty the Jones family considered the Garvey movement a primarily West Indian phenomenon.

Joe Jones moved to New York because, as his son Celedonia explains, "Everyone was moving to New York. Lots of people from Charleston had moved to Harlem." Through Ethel Peronneau, a nurse from Charleston, Joe found lodging with the Phillips family in Harlem. He did get in touch with his father, Joseph Jones Sr., who had stayed in Newark. But their relationship remained distant.

Many Harlem families, like the Phillipses, took in boarders in those days. In part, they did so to pay the high rents the mostly white landlords charged for the prime new Harlem real estate. But they also did so to fill a need. Taking in people who were not blood relatives was a long tradition among African Americans. Many blacks ran informal boarding houses in the South to provide lodging for black travelers who were denied admittance to white hotels and boarding houses.

When Joe Jones went to live with the Phillipses in Harlem, the neighborhood was almost all black. The census page on which Joe Jones is listed covers two houses on West 141st Street and forty-four people. Nine were born in New York, including four children age seven and younger, whose parents had been born elsewhere. One person was born in Connecticut, one in Sweden, and one in Cuba. There were also several people from Barbados and the Virgin Islands. The rest were southern born, from North Carolina, Alabama, and Virginia.

Probably through South Carolina connections, Joe found a job in a bakery. He changed jobs frequently, always looking for a higher wage,

Two men tighten a rivet on the side of a tunnel, which when completed would carry vehicles between New York and New Jersey, 1924. There was work aplenty for laborers in New York City.

but this was hard to find for an illiterate, unskilled transplanted southerner in Harlem. For while its population made it a black capital, in reality, according to historian William Loren Katz in *Black Legacy: A History of New York's African Americans*, "Harlem was a colony owned by absentee white landlords who controlled 80 percent of its businesses, buildings, and profit-making establishments. . . . Few white entrepreneurs in Harlem employed people of color, and those who did consigned them to menial positions."

The poet and writer Langston Hughes, who had moved to Harlem in 1921, wrote in his autobiography, *The Big Sea*: "Black Harlem really was in white face, economically speaking. So I wrote this poem:

> Because my mouth
> Is wide with laughter,
> And my throat is deep with song,
> You do not think
> I suffer after
> I have held my pain
> So long?
>
> Because my mouth
> Is wide with laughter,
> You do not hear
> My inner cry?
> Because my feet
> Are gay with dancing
> You do not know
> I die?

While living with the Phillips family, Joe met and fell in love with Augustine Phillips's younger sister, Edith. She was a hard worker, a

Edith Phillips Jones, about 1955.

*Joseph Jones in Washington, D.C.,
early 1980s.*

devout churchgoer, and a proud woman. Edith used the term *black* to describe herself, which was unusual in the days when the common term was *Negro* and the polite term was *colored*. She and Joe were married on January 26, 1922. Over the next ten years, Joe and Edith Jones had five children: Elizabeth, Pauline, Joseph, Celedonia, and Bennie.

To support his growing family, Joe Jones worked variously as a stevedore on the Brooklyn docks, as a laborer with the Pennsylvania Railroad, and as a truck driver for a market. His highest wage for any of those jobs was $30 per week. The schools his children attended were run down and overcrowded. The mostly white teachers didn't believe their students were capable of learning more than the basics of reading, writing, and math. Harlem schoolchildren were not taught about electricity, for instance, because their teachers felt they didn't have the capacity to understand it.

MEANWHILE, BRICKTOP HAD BEEN PERFORMING at Lester Mapp's club in San Francisco when peace was declared and the armistice signed on November 11, 1918. The following year brought the red summer along with the passage of the Volstead Act, which banned the sale and use of alcoholic beverages throughout the nation. With it, the period of Prohibition was underway.

More than any other event in twentieth-century United States history, Prohibition helped organized crime establish a foothold. People were not going to stop drinking because of some "silly" law. In fact, more young people started drinking in rebellion against the Volstead Act than ever before. Clubs called speakeasies quickly opened in cities across the country. One could not gain entrance without a special password, or a special friend. Before long, these establishments that sold bootleg, or illegal, liquor were operating quite openly, thanks to mob payoffs to local police. For entertainers, nothing better could have happened; a talented performer could practically pick his or her job.

Toward the end of 1922, Bricktop returned to Chicago to visit her family. "After a short, happy reunion with Mama and Blonzetta, I was itching to get out on the cabaret floor again," Bricktop said. "Prohibition was in full force by this time, and the pace of the sporting life had stepped up." In no time at all, she was off to Harlem.

A combination of Prohibition, discovery by downtown whites of the New Negro, and the creative excitement of a truly black metropolis had spawned the Harlem Renaissance. That creative rebirth included the paintings of Aaron Douglas and William H. Johnson and the sculptures of Augusta Savage; the novels of Zora Neale Hurston, Jean Toomer, and Claude McKay and the poetry of Langston Hughes and Countee Cullen. But the most popular art forms to come out of the Harlem Renaissance were music and dance.

Jazz was the most important African-American musical form to emerge. A combination of black musical styles, including slave songs, spirituals, blues, and ragtime, it was characterized by improvisation. By the end of World War I, these forms had coalesced into a distinct jazz form. As more and more blacks migrated to urban areas, jazz influences cross-fertilized. Jazz seemed to symbolize the times. Life moved faster in an era of rapid industrialization and population movement. The synchronized rhythms and improvised melodies of jazz reflected American postwar life.

Jazz music, and especially dance, made the all-black show *Shuffle Along* an immediate hit. In fact, the opening of the show at the Sixty-third Street Theatre in New York City in May 1921 is considered by many as the launching of the Harlem Renaissance. The success of *Shuffle Along* started a whole new era for blacks on Broadway, and jazz dancing became the rage. Between 1921 and 1939, some forty black musicals were staged, all with lots of dancing and a large chorus line of dancers. These black shows began the precision dancing that has been expected of show chorus lines ever since.

Shuffle Along

Shuffle Along was conceived by two teams of black entertainers—Noble Sissle and Eubie Blake, and Flournoy Miller and Aubrey Lyles. It was a combination of their respective acts and was organized around a loose plotline: the election of a mayor in all-black Jimtown, Mississippi. The entertainers had no money for sets and costumes, and when offered the use of the old Sixty-third Street Theatre, they added material based on the costumes and props they found there. The show featured the first expression of honest, tender uncomic love between a black man and a black woman on stage. It also presented several songs that would become familiar around the world, among them, "I'm Just Wild About Harry," composed by Eubie Blake.

**Words and Music by
Noble Sissle and Eubie Blake**

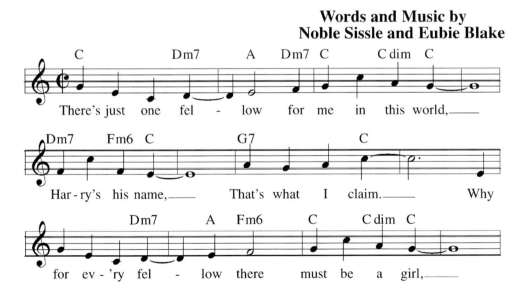

I've found my mate _____ By kind-ness of fate. _____

Chorus
I'm just wild _____ a-bout Har-ry, _____ and Har-ry's wild _____

_ a-bout me. _____ The heav'n-ly bliss - es

of his kiss - es fill me with ec - sta - sy. _____

_ He's sweet just like _____ choc'-late can dy, and

just like hon - ey from the bee. _____ Oh, I'm just wild _____

_ a-bout Har - ry, And he's just wild _____ a-bout,

can-not do _____ with-out, He's just wild _____ a-bout me. _____

Bricktop and friends, 1917. The legendary piano player Jelly Roll Morton is next to her, in bow tie.

The Cotton Club, like Barron's Exclusive Club and Connie's Inn, was an exclusive Harlem nightclub during Prohibition.

Duke Ellington, Cab Calloway, and other orchestra leaders rose to fame during the Harlem Renaissance, as did singers Lena Horne and Ethel Waters, and dancers Bill "Bojangles" Robinson and the Nicholas brothers. They performed at exclusive nightclubs in Harlem that gave white downtowners a taste of the excitement of drinking illegal liquor and experiencing first hand the so-called primitive rhythms of the New Negro.

Like so many other blacks, Bricktop was drawn to the excitement of Harlem. She got in touch with Barron Wilkins, who had nicknamed her Bricktop years earlier, was hired on the spot, and "walked into a grandstand seat at the carnival called New York in those Prohibition days. . . . Harlem was the 'in' place to go for music and booze . . ."

"Barron's was called Barron's Exclusive Club, and it *was* exclusive," Bricktop recalled. "Only light-skinned Negroes could get in, unless you happened to be someone special like Jack Johnson or the great Negro comic Bert Williams. . . . Every night the limousines pulled up to the corner of Seventh Avenue and 134th Street, and the rich whites would get out, all dolled up in their furs and jewels. Going to work at Barron's was the new high point of my career."

From Barron's, Bricktop went to Connie's Inn, a new, exclusive Harlem club, where she was a headliner. But she was restless, and when she was offered the opportunity to go to Paris as the headliner at a club called Le Grand Duc, she accepted without hesitation.

"It was a spur-of-the-moment thing, a new adventure just for the sake of adventure. I wasn't running away from anything. In fact, I was happy with my life in New York, but it turned out the timing of the move was perfect, for the glittering, happy world of the Harlem nightclubs was soon to end. When I said goodbye to Barron Wilkins, it was the last time I was to see him. Soon he would fall victim to the stepped-up competition among the bootleggers who were trying to control the Harlem trade."

When Bricktop arrived in Paris, only a handful of American blacks lived there. Among them was the poet and writer Langston Hughes, who was working as a busboy at Le Grand Duc. Most blacks were entertainers, catering to the new French interest in American jazz, to which they had been introduced during World War I. The 369th Infantry from Harlem had traveled to France with a band led by James Reese Europe, and by the time the war was over, jazz fever had seized the French. When *Shuffle Along* went on a tour of the continent, the black musical also captured the fascination of Europeans. Over the next fifteen years, hundreds of African-American entertainers would travel to Europe to perform. Like Langston Hughes before them, writers such as Claude McKay and artists such as painter Palmer Hayden and sculptor Augusta Savage found that in France they could live freer than in the United States. Josephine Baker, a young singer and dancer from East Saint Louis, Illinois, who had gotten her start in the chorus line of *Shuffle Along*, arrived in Paris not long after Bricktop and soon became the toast of the continent.

There was a substantial colony of rich white Americans in Paris, and Bricktop was soon in great demand to teach the new American dances, such as the Charleston, to them and their friends. Within a year, Le Grand Duc had become the "in place" for Americans in Paris, and Bricktop had become a self-described "saloonkeeper par excellence." She then left Le Grand Duc and opened her own club, Bricktop's.

"Everybody belonged," she said, "or else they didn't bother coming to Bricktop's more than once. When people came to Bricktop's and belonged, it was as if they were coming to one of their own salons. . . . They felt at home at Bricktop's."

Although the Great Depression was triggered by the crash of the New York stock market, its main cause was economic imbalance in the United States, including a huge disparity in the incomes of rich and poor. Arthur Rothstein captured the poverty of rural blacks in this famous photograph entitled "Gee's Bend, Alabama, 1938."

Six

The Depression Ends the Northward Flow

THE NEW YORK STOCK MARKET CRASHED IN 1929. OCTOBER 24, EVER afterward called Black Thursday, began at the New York Stock Exchange in lower Manhattan with a rush of sell orders, sending stock prices tumbling and creating a panic situation among investors. Although that event is often said to have started the Great Depression that followed, in reality it was just a symptom of the economic imbalances in the United States. A huge disparity in the incomes of rich and poor, minimal controls on the nation's money supply, and other circumstances were at fault. But the stock market crash was a frightening symbol. A severe economic slump ensued, and in just two months unemployment soared from 500,000 to over four million. Construction dropped precipitously, as did manufacturing; and because the stock market crash had shattered public confidence, practically no one was investing. The Great Depression set in; by the spring of 1935, the total of unemployed Americans had reached 15 million.

Gordon Parks, who later became a world-famous photographer, filmmaker, and writer, was sixteen years old in 1929 and working as a bellboy at an exclusive club in Saint Paul, Minnesota. In his autobiography, he recalled how the stock market crash changed his life:

'MARKET CRASHES—PANIC HITS NATION!' one headline blared. The newspapers were full of it, and I read everything I could get my hands on, gathering in the full meaning of such terms as Black Thursday, deflation and depression. I couldn't imagine such financial disaster touching my small world; it surely concerned only the rich. But by the first week of November I too knew differently; along with millions of others across the nation, I was without a job.

Although the Depression affected nearly every American, it was particularly hard on blacks, and especially on those who had moved to northern cities from the South. The Great Migration had continued throughout the 1920s. Between 1920 and 1930, more than 800,000 southern blacks had moved north. The black populations of New York, Chicago, and Cleveland had doubled; that of Detroit had tripled. When the Depression came, urban blacks found themselves in dire straits.

The Harlem Renaissance ended as the Great Depression took root. The repeal of the Volstead Act in December 1933 meant that organized crime lost its very profitable illegal liquor business. Mobsters vied for control of other illegal activities, such as drugs and gambling. Increasing gang violence cast a pall on Harlem, and the big nightclubs either closed or moved downtown. Harlem was no longer a playground; it was a sad and dangerous place. There had always been poverty and despair in

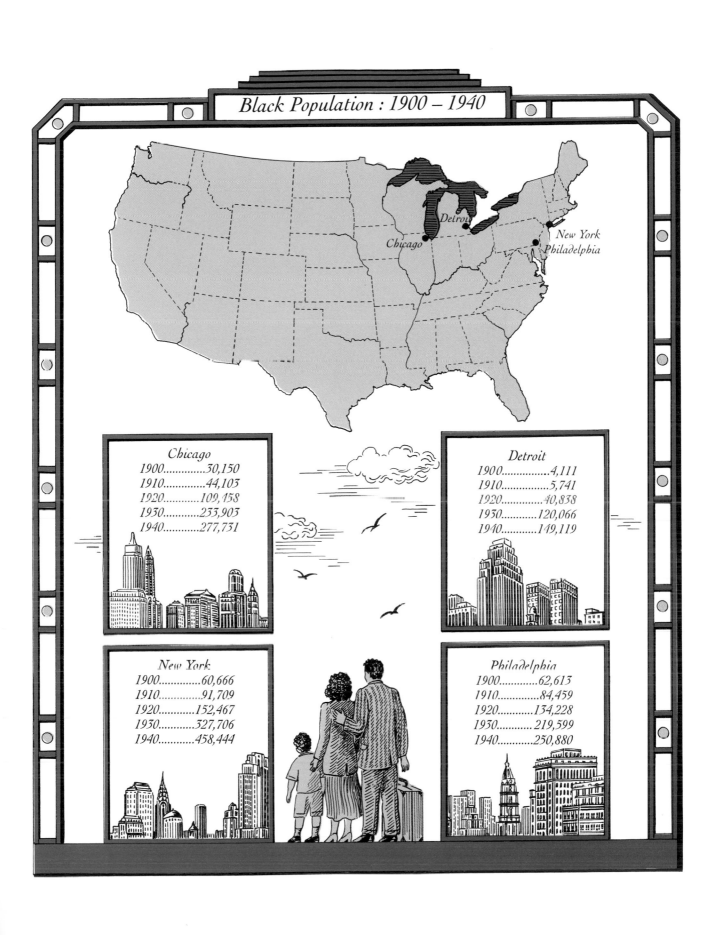

Black Population : 1900 – 1940

Chicago
1900............30,150
1910............44,103
1920...........109,158
1930...........233,903
1940...........277,731

Detroit
1900.............4,111
1910.............5,741
1920............40,838
1930..........120,066
1940..........149,119

New York
1900............60,666
1910............91,709
1920...........152,467
1930...........327,706
1940...........458,444

Philadelphia
1900............62,613
1910............84,459
1920...........134,228
1930...........219,599
1940...........250,880

Men playing checkers on Lenox Avenue, New York City. During the Great Depression, the black unemployment rate was much worse than the white.

Harlem, but for outsiders it had been masked by the high life of the clubs and the myth of the singing and dancing New Negro. Now, there was nothing to cloak its misery.

Many of the artists, writers, and performers who had helped create the Harlem Renaissance moved away; ironically, several went south. W. E. B. Du Bois accepted a professorship at Atlanta University. Painter Aaron Douglas went to Fisk University, the all-black college in Nashville, Tennessee. Those who remained had a hard time finding work. Blacks, as the saying went, were always "last hired and first fired," and the unemployment rate for blacks during the Great Depression was considerably worse than for whites. By 1935, wages for Harlemites were 46 percent lower than those of the white poor. Yet the city's Home Relief Bureau provided fewer services to Harlem than to other areas. As an example, while blacks constituted 21 percent of the people on relief, they received only 9 percent of work relief jobs. Migration of southern blacks to Harlem and other northern cities fell to its lowest point in thirty years. In Chicago, the *Defender* for the first time began advising southern blacks to stay home.

Joe Jones struggled to take care of his growing family. They were living at 2903 Eighth Avenue between 153rd and 154th Streets in Harlem when the stock market crashed, but in 1930, not long after the birth of their fourth child, Celedonia, they relocated to 563 Rockaway Avenue in the Brownsville section of Brooklyn, where Joe hoped to find work on the Brooklyn waterfront.

According to his son Celedonia, Joe would go out in the morning and stand near the docks along with dozens of other laborers, in what was called a shape-up. If a man looked strong and healthy and "in good shape," he might be hired as a day laborer on the docks. But work was not guaranteed, and the wages were low. The Joneses sought other ways to care for their family.

"My father was always on the lookout for ways to get money or

Countee Cullen, Teacher

After the Harlem Renaissance ended, Countee Cullen continued to publish, turning from poetry to novels. But he could not support himself by his writing. He went to work as a teacher of English and French at Public School 139 in Harlem. Among his students was Joe Jones's son Celedonia.

The mild-mannered Cullen encouraged his students to defend their work and to try to persuade him to give them a higher grade, and his students rose to the challenge. One time, the assignment was an essay on an event in history. Celedonia Jones received a 75 and argued that he should have gotten an 85. Cullen changed the grade, adding, "You could have gotten a 90 if you had done more research." "History doesn't interest me," Jones responded. Cullen looked at him gravely. "When you take more interest in yourself," he said, "you will become more interested in history." That advice lay dormant in Celedonia Jones's mind for years.

"Boy seated with a paper." As a youngster in Depression-era Harlem, Joe Jones's son Celedonia remembers missing many meals and moving frequently to avoid being evicted from apartments.

whatever else we needed," says Celedonia. Accordingly, in 1932, Joe Jones applied to the Veterans Administration for disability payments, citing problems with his teeth that had occurred during his army service and for which he had received dental care in Bordeaux, France. Because Joe was illiterate, his wife, Edith, filled out the application for disability on his behalf. Joe was denied veterans disability payments, but the application, still in the files of the United States Veterans Administration, contains a great deal of information about Joe Jones, his family, and his various jobs.

The Great Depression spurred the growth of a number of religious sects among blacks, whose despair caused them to seek solace outside established churches. George Baker of Savannah, Georgia, who had migrated to New York City in the late 1910s, rose to the height of his fame during this time. Calling himself God, or Father Divine, and his wife Mother Divine, he established a series of storefront chapels called peace missions that handed out generous meals for pennies. By 1935, he had enrolled a large, interracial congregation that numbered anywhere from half a million to two million, depending on the source, who worshipped him as God incarnate. Generous donations from those followers enabled Father Divine to purchase fifteen buildings in New York City alone, as well as buildings in other New York City boroughs, suburbs of the city, New Jersey, Connecticut, and Washington, D.C.

In the Brooklyn area, where the Jones family lived, a local church called the Moorish Science Temple provided food and other support for its parishioners. The Jones family joined that church, whose members added the suffix "Bey" to their last names. Thus, the Jones family became the Jones-Bey family. Celedonia Jones remembers that when he was enrolled in kindergarten, he was known as Celedonia Jones-Bey and he had Fridays off because of his religion.

Celedonia Jones recalls, "At the Moorish Science Temple, there was a Grand Sheik and a Grand Sheikess, and they dressed in Arabian-style

Father Divine attracted a great number of followers, who worshipped him as God incarnate on Earth. He established a Peace Mission in Harlem, which served as both a church and a soup kitchen. Celedonia Jones remembers going there for meals.

clothes with bloomer-type pants. My father was quite a dresser, and we took to calling him The Sheik."

The Jones family stayed in Brooklyn about five years. After a time, Joe Jones decided that living there was downright risky. Longshoremen gangs controlled the docks at this time and decided who would get work. Joe later told his children that the gangs also controlled the local loan-sharking business, lending money at a high rate of interest—"one hundred cents on the dollar," Joe would say. Joe soon learned that if a man owed money to the gangs, he was more likely to be picked for day work: "Those who had a little tab [loan] could get work because then they could pay the loan back," Celedonia Jones explains. So, Joe took out a loan; but then he found he could not repay it. Those who could not pay back their loans were beaten up and their families threatened. Joe moved his family back to Manhattan.

Over the next several years, the family lived in Harlem and moved almost annually—"one step before dispossession, because we couldn't pay the rent," says Celedonia Jones. "There were many missed meals. My father was not much of a provider, but he was very much a protector. I remember when we lived in Brooklyn, a teacher hit my sister, and the whole school could hear my father yelling, 'You don't touch my child!'"

"There were five of us children, and my father would make a fist and say, 'What one finger can't do, a fist can,' by which he meant that we should look out for one another. He'd say, 'If one of you comes home crying, you'd better *all* come home crying.'"

By the time the Jones family returned to Harlem, President Franklin D. Roosevelt had instituted a number of measures to help lift the nation out of the Great Depression. Using the term *New Deal* to describe his program, he persuaded Congress to pass legislation creating a variety of efforts to provide work, such as the Farm Security Administration, the Work Projects Administration, and the Federal Arts Project. Federal, state, and local governments created Home Relief programs to provide

Federal, state, and local governments instituted measures to help people suffering from the effects of the Great Depression. New York City set up unemployment relief offices, and so many men lined up to register that police reserves were called in to keep order.

basic living assistance. Large, private institutions also established programs to provide food and other assistance.

The Jones family took advantage of whatever help they could find. Celedonia remembers going to Father Divine's peace mission for meals. He also remembers dressing in government-issue clothing. "You could always tell which kids were on relief," says Celedonia, "because the government-issue shirts didn't have pockets."

By 1938, the children were all in school, and Edith Phillips Jones went to work to augment the family income. She was employed variously as a nanny for white children and as a housekeeper. The housekeeping work was primarily day work. Early in the morning, she would take the subway up to Fulton Street in the Bronx. White women from Westchester County and parts of the Bronx would drive by and stop when they saw a likely worker. Often, they would get out of the car and feel a woman's muscles to see if she was capable of doing a good day's work. "They would set the clock back on her," says Celedonia Jones, meaning that just before it was time for Edith Jones to leave, the mistress of the house would change the clock to show an earlier hour so she could get more work out of her one-day maid. "Or," adds Celedonia Jones, "just before she was ready to leave, they'd bring out the silver to shine— a half hour job."

IN THE MEANTIME, the effects of the stock market crash and the Depression in the United States had taken a while to be felt in Europe. Bricktop, who had married Peter Duconge, a saxophone player from New Orleans, on December 29, 1929, just two months after the crash, recalled, "Only a handful of my clients were affected immediately and suddenly disappeared from Paris. Others who hadn't been wiped out kept telling one another that it was only a temporary crisis, and that in a few weeks there would be a turn for the better."

Unconcerned about what was happening across the Atlantic, the

Duconges purchased an estate outside of Paris. "With the times what they were, with the economy across the Atlantic so rocky, I should have cut down—hoarded my francs and behaved like a normal businesswoman with cash on her hands instead of bills. But I decided to open a bigger club," Bricktop later said.

By the fall of 1933, business at Bricktop's had dropped precipitously. "Some nights the club was less than half full. People who never had a prayer of getting into Bricktop's in the big years had no trouble getting in now," Bricktop recalled. She had to give up the big club and open a smaller place. By the fall of 1936, she didn't have enough money for her own club and went to work for someone else.

Unable to find work, many other African-American entertainers had left Europe by that time. As Germany and its ally Italy began to annex surrounding territories, others returned home for fear of being caught in the German steamroller. All foreigners would be subject to internment in concentration camps, and black foreigners would face particular hardships from a conquering nation that hated all non-Aryans. But Bricktop stayed on. Her mother had died back in the United States in 1938; she was separated from Peter Duconge; she had lived in Paris since 1924 and considered it her home.

But after Germany invaded Poland on September 1, 1939, and England and France declared war on Germany two days later, Bricktop realized she had no choice but to leave. She managed to book passage on one of the last American ships to leave France in late October 1939. She was forty-five years old.

By the time Bricktop returned to New York, the Great Migration had ended. During the Great Depression, migration of southern blacks to northern cities fell to the lowest point in thirty years. But the Depression was also on the wane, due largely to the outbreak of World War II in Europe. Although the United States had every intention of staying out of World War II, President Franklin D. Roosevelt had

Bricktop, center, at Bricktop's in Paris, surrounded by clients and friends. Louis Bromfield, one of her favorite clients, is at center. Bromfield's secretary, Jack Hawkins, is seated with Bricktop. At far right is the British singer Mabel Mercer, arm in arm with Marjorie Oelrichs, a famous society beauty.

promised to help American allies in Europe, and U.S. industry was humming with production of war matériel for England and France. The United States eventually entered the war in 1941, and the booming factories spurred yet another wave of black migration, one that would rise to the highest point ever reached, at some 150,000 per year.

Girls listen to their grandmother, who passes her story on.

Seven

Legacy of the Great Migration

THE PARTICIPANTS IN THE GREAT MIGRATION HAD LEFT "THE DARKNESS of the South" behind. They would never again have to suffer being called "Boy" and "Girl" rather than "Mister" and "Miss." They would not have to cross to the other side of the street when they saw white people approaching, or suffer the indignity of searching desperately for a "colored" rest room or water fountain. They would not have to give up their bus seats to whites. They would not have to pass by the bodies of dead men hanging from trees, lynched by white mobs for "crimes" as minor as looking directly at a white woman. Black women were no longer vulnerable to rape and exploitation by white men because too many southern whites considered all blacks their collective property. Black children could attend school for as many months as white children did and not according to white landowners' crop schedules. Northern blacks enjoyed the right to vote and exercised that right, with the result that in some northern cities like Chicago and New York, they held the balance of power in close municipal elections.

But there was a downside to living in the North. Rapid settlement of southern and foreign blacks in northern cities coincided with the migration of whites away from the cities or to less populated areas of the cities. In Harlem, in the decade between 1920 and 1930, 118,792 white people moved out, and 87,417 blacks moved in. As in black sections in other cities, such as the South Side of Chicago, many of the homes the whites left behind had deteriorated, but blacks were so desperate for housing that they moved into whatever homes they could find. Those black sections rapidly became slums—their housing, schools, and employment opportunities worse than in the cities overall and their levels of crime, disease, and mortality higher. There was no legalized segregation in the North, but de facto segregation, or segregation in fact, was all too real.

As an example, white real estate agents refused to show houses in white areas to prospective black homeowners because they knew whites in those areas worried that the arrival of blacks would reduce the value of their properties. Even the Federal Housing Authority would not provide mortgages for blacks moving into white neighborhoods because the future value of homes owned by blacks was uncertain. Segregated housing resulted in segregated schools.

Black northerners fought against the conditions that kept them down. In large numbers, black workers campaigned for inclusion in the growing labor movement. Convinced that the limited government efforts to relieve African-American poverty during the Great Depression made an alliance with the white labor movement necessary, A. Philip Randolph, president of the all-black Brotherhood of Sleeping Car Porters (BSCP), which by 1935 numbered some 35,000 members, stepped up efforts to make the labor movement interracial. In 1936, the BSCP won full rights as an independent union of the American Federation of Labor. That same year, Randolph helped found and became president of the

A. Phillip Randolph speaks at the Lincoln Memorial.

National Negro Congress (NNC), a federation of existing labor and civil rights organizations. Its first convention in Chicago attracted delegates from 585 organizations.

In addition to pushing for inclusion in the labor movement, the NNC initiated and coordinated seventy regional councils that focused on local issues of discrimination. The Chicago council emphasized jobs, conducted rent strikes for better housing on the city's South Side, and urged more public relief for the city's blacks. In New York, the NNC backed the Greater New York Coordinating Committee for Employment, led by the Reverend Adam Clayton Powell Jr., which campaigned for a third of all retail jobs in Harlem to be filled by African Americans. Powell, using his base as pastor of the Abyssinian Baptist Church, became the most

Congressman Adam C. Powell addresses a large crowd in front of the White House.

important black political figure in the city and in 1944 was the first African American from New York State elected to Congress.

In the meantime, some 60 percent of African Americans continued to live in the South, where mechanization created even less need for their work on the region's farms and where legal segregation, poverty, lack of education, and denial of all dignity eventually inspired the direct-action civil rights movement. It was a movement that had little impact in the North, where the influence of the church was not as strong and where segregation did not exist by law. Not until the Black Power movement of the late 1960s and 1970s was the influence of northern blacks felt in great numbers.

EACH PARTICIPANT IN THE GREAT MIGRATION WAS UNIQUE, and the story of each is distinct. Bricktop and Joe Jones, the two people whose stories you have followed in these pages, migrated to the North for similar reasons, but they went to two different cities at two different times. They also had very diverse experiences, both during and after the years of the Great Migration. You have learned of their experiences during this time. This is what happened to them afterward:

On her return to the United States in 1939, Bricktop hoped to establish a Bricktop's in New York City. Many of her former clients in Paris had relocated there, among them the songwriter Cole Porter, who threw a big party to welcome her at his apartment in the exclusive Waldorf Towers. Arriving at the Waldorf Towers on her second night back in New York, Bricktop recalled in her autobiography,

I walked smack into my first taste of prejudice in the America of 1939. When I asked the receptionist for Cole's apartment, he looked me over as though he'd never seen a Negro woman before. "Are you expected?" he asked in a pained tone of voice. I told him that I thought I was. "What's your name?" he wanted to know.

Bricktop in her late eighties. Her autobiography, Bricktop, *was published in 1983, about six months before she died.*

"Miss Bricktop," I answered very quietly. Well, that changed things in a second. He came running out from behind his desk, bowing and scraping. . . . By the time I got upstairs, I was boiling mad.

In addition to racial discrimination, an anonymity to which she was unaccustomed prevented Bricktop from recapturing the magic of the Paris Bricktop's. Bankrolled by the tobacco heiress Doris Duke, she relocated to Mexico City.

But she still considered Europe her real home, and in 1950, after World War II ended, she returned to Paris and opened another Bricktop's. The rampant postwar anti-Americanism there appalled her, however, and she moved on to Rome, Italy. There, from 1951 until 1965, she reigned as nightclub queen of the city that was called Hollywood-on-the-Tiber because of its large American film colony. "I did quite a bit of moving around during that part of my life," Bricktop wrote in her auto-biography. "People ask me now, 'What were you looking for?' I was looking for Bricktop's." But she never found it.

Bricktop's last major engagement was in New York, where she hosted a Bricktop Hour at the club 21 in 1979. She was living in New York at that time and began to collaborate with Jim Haskins on her life story, *Bricktop*, which was published in August 1983, on her eighty-ninth birthday. She died in her sleep on January 31, 1984. Bricktop had no children.

In 1939, the same year that Bricktop arrived back in New York from Paris, Joe and Edith Jones separated; they would never divorce. Joe was in his midforties. For the next forty-plus years, he moved from place to place. Both he and Bricktop had restless spirits—understandable, perhaps, for people who had been part of the Great Migration. After Edith Jones died in 1970, Joe remarried twice. Both marriages were brief; Joe was too protective of his freedom. When he split up with his third wife, he was eighty-four years old.

By that time, Joe was going blind and could not care for himself. Through the efforts of his son Celedonia he was admitted to a Veterans Administration Extended Care Center facility in Saint Albans, Queens, New York. He entered the center when he was eighty-nine and died the following year at age ninety.

Unlike Bricktop, Joe Jones left five children. They and their parents had gone through hard times; but they had survived and prospered. All of the children finished high school, and some earned college degrees. Joe Jones's fourth child and second son, Celedonia, worked as a licensed public accountant for various municipal agencies; his last paying job was in the office of the comptroller of the City of New York.

The words of his junior high school English teacher, Countee Cullen, had stayed in the back of Celedonia Jones's mind, and half a century later, on his retirement, he determined to find his own history. He began to research his family, sending away for birth, death, and military

Celedonia Jones is sworn in as Manhattan Borough Historian, January 1997.

records; visiting libraries, archives, and government records offices up and down the eastern seaboard; and searching through miles of micro-filmed census material. He then started on his wife's family and managed to trace her father's line back to 1791. Through these efforts, Jones became a highly regarded, self-taught historian, and in January 1997 he was appointed to the position of Manhattan Borough Historian. Manhattan Borough President Ruth Messinger chose him for this hon-orary position, and Messinger's successor as borough president, C. Virginia Fields, continued Jones's appointment.

Like the children of Joe Jones, most of the children of the Great Migration persevered and survived—and some thrived. They got jobs, earned college degrees, and entered professions that had previously been closed to them. They exercised their power of the vote and elected African Americans as mayors and other high officials of major cities. Although even the most educated and well-to-do are subject from time to time to discrimination, both subtle and obvious, northern urban blacks have made their cities their homes—and themselves a force to be reckoned with.

Bibliography

American Social History Project. *Who Built America?* Vol. 2, *From the Gilded Age to the Present*. New York: American Social History Productions and Pantheon Books, 1972.

Anderson, Jervis. *This Was Harlem: A Cultural Portrait, 1900–1950*. New York: Farrar, Straus, & Giroux, 1982.

Bricktop, with James Haskins. *Bricktop*. New York: Atheneum, 1983.

Groh, George W. *The Black Migration: The Journey to Urban America*. New York: Weybright and Talley, 1972.

Grossman, James R. *A Chance to Make Good: African Americans, 1900–1929*. New York: Oxford University Press, 1997.

Henri, Florette. *Black Migration: Movement North, 1900–1920*. Garden City, NY: Anchor Press/Doubleday, 1975.

Hughes, Langston. *The Big Sea: An Autobiography*. New York: Alfred A. Knopf, 1940.

Jackson, Florence. *The Black Man in America, 1905–1932*. New York: Franklin Watts, 1974.

Katz, William Loren. *Black Legacy: A History of New York's African Americans*. New York: Atheneum Books for Young Readers, 1997.

Locke, Alain, ed. *The New Negro: An Interpretation*. New York: A. and C. Boni, 1925.

Meltzer, Milton. *The Black Americans: A History in Their Own Words, 1619–1983*. New York: Thomas Y. Crowell, 1984.

Osofsky, Gilbert. *Harlem—The Making of a Ghetto: Negro New York, 1890–1930*. New York: Harper & Row, 1966.

Parks, Gordon. *A Choice of Weapons*. New York: Harper & Row, 1966.

Further Reading

Grossman, James R. *A Chance to Make Good: African Americans, 1900–1929*. New York: Oxford University Press, 1997.

Harding, Vincent. *We Changed the World: African Americans, 1945–1970*. New York: Oxford University Press, 1997.

Haskins, James. *Black Music in America: A History Through Its People*. New York: HarperCollins Publishers, 1987.

Haskins, James. *Black Theater in America*. New York: Thomas Y. Crowell, 1982.

Haskins, Jim. *The Harlem Renaissance*. Brookfield, CT: The Millbrook Press, 1996.

Katz, William Loren. *Black Legacy: A History of New York's African Americans*. New York: Atheneum, 1997.

Index